WOMEN WHO WON'T BE SILENCED

THE STORIES OF STRONG WOMEN

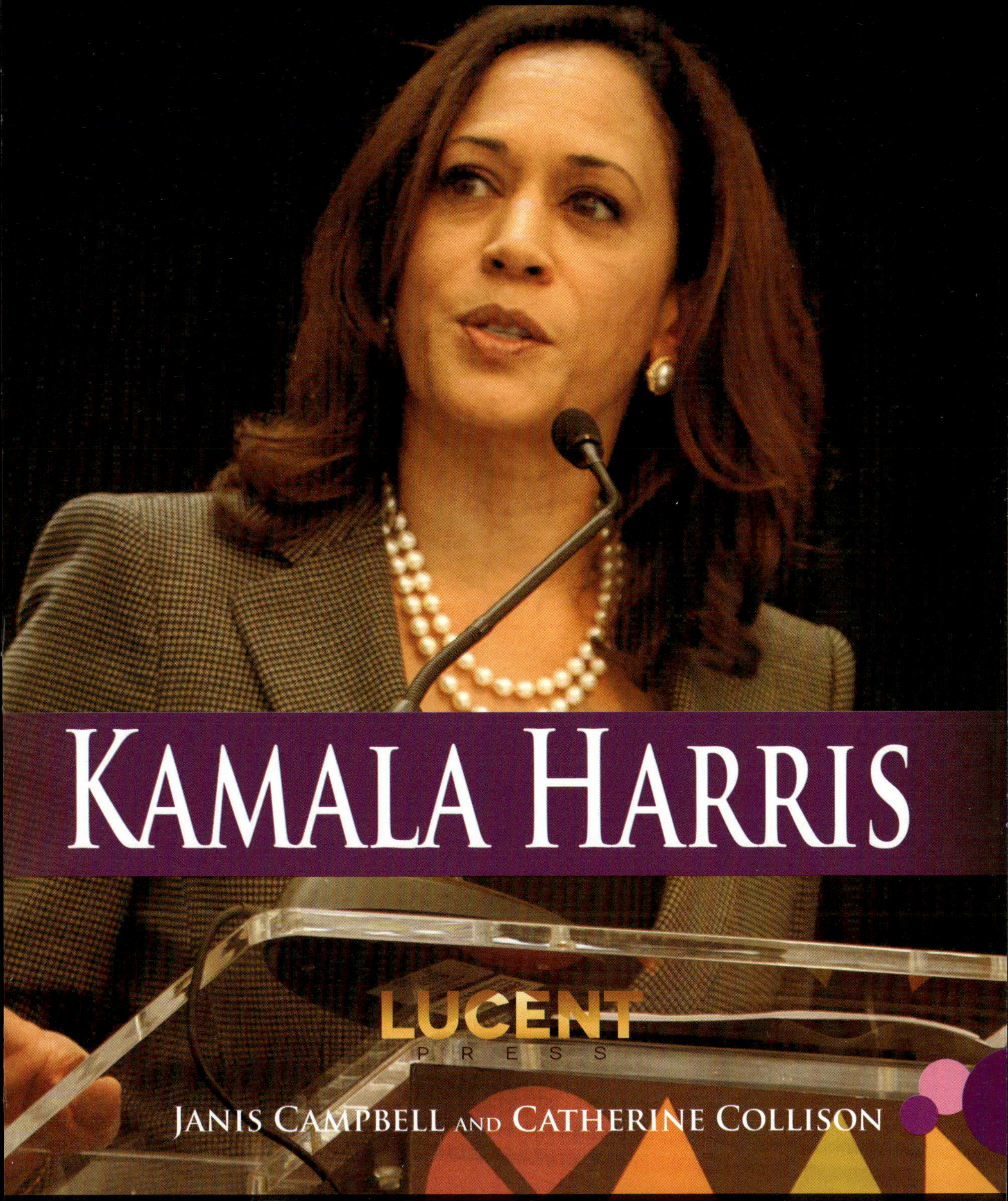

KAMALA HARRIS

LUCENT PRESS

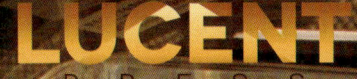

JANIS CAMPBELL AND CATHERINE COLLISON

Published in 2019 by
Lucent Press, an Imprint of Greenhaven Publishing, LLC
353 3rd Avenue
Suite 255
New York, NY 10010

Copyright © 2019 Lucent Press, an Imprint of Greenhaven Publishing, LLC.

All rights reserved. No part of this book may be reproduced in any form without permission in writing from the publisher, except by a reviewer.

Developed and produced for Rosen by BlueApple*Works* Inc.

Managing Editor for BlueApple*Works*: Melissa McClellan
Designer: Tibor Choleva
Photo Research: Jane Reid
Editor: Marcia Abramson

Photo Credits: cover DFree/Shutterstock.com; title page, p. 8, 19, 24 Office of Attorney General Kamala Harris/Public Domain; background Vladitto/Shutterstock; p.4 United States Senate/Public Domain; p. 7, 40, 46, 47, 52, 55 Office of Senator Kamala Harris/Public Domain; p. 10 Nick St. Charles/Creative Commons; p. 12–13, 14, 18, 21, 22, 25, 26–27, 28, 30, 31, 45 Office of the Attorney General of California/Public Domain; p. 17 4johnny5/Creative Commons; p. 29 Andy Dean Photography/Shutterstock; p. 33 California Department of Corrections/Public Domain; p. 34, 49, 50 Mobilus/Creative Commons; p. 36 Jeff Malet/ZUMAPRESS.com; p. 38–39 Tom Williams/Keystone Press; p. 41 Iryna Imago/Shutterstock; p. 43 California National Guard/Creative Commons; p. 44 Lorie Shaull/Creative Commons; p. 51 Sarah Reingewirtz/Keystone Press; p. 56 Featureflash Photo Agency/Shutterstock.com

Cataloging-in-Publication-Data
Names: Campbell, Janis. | Collison, Catherine.
Title: Kamala Harris / Janis Campbell and Catherine Collison.
Description: New York : Lucent Press, 2019. | Series: Women who won't be silenced: the stories of strong women | Includes glossary and index.
Identifiers: ISBN 9781534566507 (pbk.) | ISBN 9781534566514 (library bound) | ISBN 9781534566521 (ebook)
Subjects: LCSH: Harris, Kamala D. -- Juvenile literature. | African American politicians -- Biography -- Juvenile literature. | African American lawyers--Biography--Juvenile literature.
Classification: LCC E185.96 C67 2019 | DDC 324.092'396073 B--dc23

Manufactured in the United States of America

CPSIA Compliance Information: Batch #BW19KL: For Further Information contact: Greenhaven Publishing LLC, New York, New York at 1-844-317-7404.

CONTENTS

Chapter 1
Who Is Kamala D. Harris?.. 4

Chapter 2
Childhood and Education 8

Chapter 3
San Francisco's District Attorney 14

Chapter 4
Attorney General of California 22

Chapter 5
California's Third Female U.S. Senator 34

Chapter 6
Future Plans 52

Recognition 58

Timeline 60

Glossary 62

For More Information 63

Index 64

CHAPTER 1

WHO IS KAMALA D. HARRIS?

Kamala D. Harris is a fierce fighter, devoted to standing up and speaking out for others. She is not one to shy away from a fight if the cause is just and right.

When Kamala Harris ran for the United States Senate in 2016, her campaign slogan was "Fearless for the People." That slogan describes her life and career perfectly as a woman who has dedicated her life to taking on battles for social justice, civil rights, and any issue that leaves people without help, hope, or a voice. She's unafraid in approaching people or companies when she's seeking justice.

Born on the West Coast in Oakland, California, she was introduced to civil rights and social justice at a young age. She went to the East Coast for college, where she attended historic Howard University in Washington, D.C.

She returned home to California for law school at the University of California, Hastings College of the Law. From the very beginning she followed a path of public service, working as an attorney and prosecutor before being elected as district attorney of the city and county of San Francisco for two terms.

Later, she was elected twice as attorney general for California. In 2016, she won election as a U.S. senator representing California. She began serving her six-year term in January of 2017.

Senator Harris is a determined, hardworking trailblazer. As noted on her website, she is "the second African-American woman and first South Asian-American senator in history."

With a long and distinguished legal career, and a strong voice as a new senator, she's already being mentioned as a potential contender in the 2020 presidential race. That's really no surprise given her devotion to serving the public and her dynamic personality.

"WE THE PEOPLE UNDERSTAND OUR UNITY IS OUR STRENGTH AND OUR DIVERSITY IS OUR POWER."

— Attorney General Kamala Harris, in a speech at the 2016 California Democratic Party Convention

Activism has always been part of Kamala's life. She tells a family story of how once when she was fussing as a toddler, her mom asked what she wanted and she replied: "Fweedom!" As a grown-up, she attended and spoke at a June 2014 celebration in Los Angeles of the 50th anniversary of the Civil Rights Act.

CHAPTER 2

CHILDHOOD AND EDUCATION

You could say Kamala Devi Harris was born at precisely the right time, in the right place, and to the right parents to help shape her into the leader she is today. The senator was born in Oakland, California, on October 20, 1964.

Her parents were graduate students at the nearby University of California, Berkeley, a campus buzzing with political activity and student activism in the 1960s. Her mother, Shyamala Gopalan Harris, a student from India, earned a Ph.D. in nutrition and endocrinology at UC Berkeley, and became a renowned scientist and breast cancer researcher. Her father, Donald Harris, an economics student from Jamaica, earned his Ph.D. in 1966, and was a professor of economics at prestigious Stanford University in Palo Alto. Her parents were not only scholars, but also actively engaged in the Civil Rights Movement.

Kamala's sister Maya (left) is also a lawyer and a public policy advocate, as well as an analyst with MSNBC.

Issues of social justice and activism became part of Kamala's life, too, even as a toddler. In fact, on her U.S. Senate website, she shares that she "had a stroller's-eye view of the Civil Rights Movement" which was taking center stage at Berkeley and in Oakland, as well as on college campuses and in cities across the country.

Kamala has a younger sister, Maya, who was born in 1967. Although their parents divorced when they were young, both girls celebrated their family heritage and culture. They also visited Jamaica and traveled to India many times.

Kamala and her sister moved to Canada when their mother accepted a job in Montreal, in Canada's Quebec province. Her mother was a distinguished breast cancer researcher at the Lady Davis Institute for Medical Research at the Jewish General Hospital and Department of Medicine at McGill University in Montreal. After high school, Kamala moved to Washington, D.C., to attend Howard University. She has often cited her years at Howard, where she studied political science and economics, as ones that were extremely important to shaping the path she has followed.

After graduating with a B.A. in 1986, she attended law school at the University of California, Hastings College of the Law, in San Francisco, earning her Juris Doctor degree (law degree) in 1989. She passed the state bar exam and was admitted to the California bar in 1990. Kamala Devi Harris was on her way!

"WHEN I WAS GROWING UP, MANY OF YOU MAY KNOW, MY PARENTS WERE ACTIVISTS IN THE CIVIL RIGHTS MOVEMENT. AND THERE'S SOMETHING I REMEMBER FROM MY CHILDHOOD THAT REALLY MADE ME BELIEVE IN THE POSSIBILITIES OF OUR COUNTRY. I SAW PEOPLE OF ALL AGES, ALL COLORS, ALL RELIGIONS, ALL BACKGROUNDS, UNIFIED IN THEIR FIGHT FOR JUSTICE."

– Attorney General Kamala Harris's speech at the 2016 California Democratic Party Convention as shared on her website blog

"CHILDREN ARE OUR NATION'S FUTURE. WE MUST LISTEN TO THEM ABOUT WHAT THEY CARE ABOUT AND GIVE THEM A VOICE IN OUR GOVERNMENT."

– Office of Senator Kamala Harris / Twitter / August 24, 2017

12

EARLY START

Kamala Harris had her first election victory when she was a freshman at Howard University in Washington, D.C. She shared that fact in a 2017 commencement address at the university, saying: "It prepared me for a career in public service, starting with my first-ever political race – for freshman class representative on what was then called the Liberal Arts Student Council."

Harris led many investigations as a prosecutor serving the public and plans to continue doing so as a senator. Her office says she "will follow the facts wherever they may lead to get the truth for the American people."

CHAPTER 3

SAN FRANCISCO'S DISTRICT ATTORNEY

It didn't take long for Kamala Harris to make an impact as a lawyer. If you were casting a TV series with a young, savvy lawyer taking on tough criminal cases in the district attorney's office, you would cast Harris.

Unlike TV, she's the real deal. Her work in the 1990s for the Alameda County District Attorney's Office gained attention as she prosecuted tough cases involving sexual assaults on children. In 1998, when Harris took on a new job in San Francisco's district attorney's office, that meant more tough cases. As her website notes, she also led the San Francisco City Attorney's Division on Children and Families.

"YOU DON'T HAVE TO CARE ABOUT CHILDREN TO CARE ABOUT CHILDREN. ONE OF THE THINGS THAT I TALK A LOT ABOUT IS THE FACT OF THE IMPORTANCE OF THIRD-GRADE READING LEVEL. BY THE END OF THIRD GRADE, IF THE CHILD IS NOT AT READING LEVEL, IT'LL DROP OFF. THEY NEVER CATCH UP."

– Kamala Harris, interview with Doreen St. Félix, www.elle.com. October 23, 2015.

That meant she was active in prosecuting cases of child abuse. She also paid extra attention to children who missed school, or were truant.

She got tough on prosecuting the parents for truancy. It worked – people changed their behaviors when they thought they might face time in jail for not getting their kids in school.

In 2003, she became the district attorney of the city and county of San Francisco. Harris was vigilant in her defense of the vulnerable, especially children who were harmed in assaults. She was tough on **hate crimes**.

And she was relentless when it came to prosecuting criminals who raped women.

You might think prosecutors who claim to be tough on crime would be lacking concern for the criminals they prosecute. However, Harris was a leader who balanced the need for safety with the need for solutions that went beyond putting people in prison. Her Back on Track program aims to help nonviolent offenders get educated or trained for jobs, instead of being stuck in a cycle that sent people back to prison, often after repeating their crime. Harris also called

BACK ON TRACK

The Back on Track program in San Francisco is an initiative that Kamala Harris launched in 2005 when she was the district attorney for San Francisco and San Francisco County. As she notes in her book, *Smart on Crime*, it led with a way to work with nonviolent people, ones that were "first-time drug offenders."

Getting back on track is an expression that is used when you have gotten off course, following a bad path that gets you off track in your work, school, or everyday living. The program offers a way for the courts to get people back on a lawful track. It includes community service, help with daily living, and continuing education or job training. Back on Track has won praise across the country since it began and other communities have added similar programs.

Harris celebrated with the graduating class of the San Francisco Back on Track program in 2009. More than 90 percent of the program's graduates stay on track!

17

for accountability in police departments.

Senator Harris shared her unique views and approach on crime in April 2018 with the Rev. Al Sharpton at the National Action Network convention in New York City and the interview aired on *Politics Nation* on MSNBC. Harris explained that justice requires an understanding that every police officer's family always wonders if that officer will return at the end of the shift. At the same time, she stressed that she also knows every African American man has faced discrimination and has reason to fear for himself, too, when facing police. Do you think it is possible to balance helping victims of crime, preventing crime, and making sure criminals are treated fairly? Can all these goals

As attorney general, Harris worked closely with local, state, and federal officers to get drugs, guns, and gangs off the streets. Dozens of police joined her in 2011 to announce the success of Operation Red Zone, which led to the arrests of 101 gang members in central California.

In all of her roles, Harris has visited schools often to find out what kids think and encourage them to dream big. In 2014, for example, she talked with students on the first day of school at Baldwin Hills Elementary in Los Angeles.

be accomplished?

HATE CRIME CRACKDOWN

One kind of crime that Kamala Harris has no tolerance for now – or ever – is a hate crime. As a district attorney, she prosecuted people who picked on others or assaulted them because of race, gender, religion, or sexual orientation. She was particularly passionate when **LGBT** teens had been the victims of such behavior. She continues to speak out today

19

on behalf of teens who are bullied, especially if it's about their sexual orientation.

A BOOK OF SOLUTIONS

Smart on Crime: A Career Prosecutor's Plan to Make Us Safer is the book Kamala Harris wrote with Joan O'C. Hamilton. It was published in 2009 but is still very relevant today. The book tackles crime and ways to make communities safer. Harris writes about Back on Track and other programs she has been involved with, such as her successful effort to reduce elementary school truancy by cracking down on parents or guardians who don't get their kids to school.

A main premise of the book is that your safety is your right. You have a right to be safe from crime, safe on the street, safe in your home, and safe at school. And you also have the right to be safe if speaking out or protesting. The book is both optimistic in tone and practical in offering solutions. It lays out key support for programs that counties or cities cannot afford to ignore, programs that Harris stresses would ensure better outcomes for all. It also talks about making sure budgets include these programs,

As a California attorney general, Harris issued regular reports on school truancy and efforts to tackle the problem. She chose John Muir Elementary in San Francisco as the place to release her 2016 report and visited with students as well.

because it's better to pay more to prevent crime than to just pay the costs of crime later.

The preface of the book also shares some personal remembrances of Harris's childhood, and her heritage. She credits her parents' early years as planting the seed for her passion for justice, as well as her heritage, especially her Indian grandmother, and coming from a family with a passion for public service.

Check it out at your library. What ideas might work in your town? Maybe you have more ideas of your own!

Kamala Harris's official photograph as California attorney general.

CHAPTER 4

ATTORNEY GENERAL OF CALIFORNIA

It's pretty rare for an election to be so close that a winner isn't made clear on election night. It's even more unusual for a candidate to declare victory and then later have to concede a loss. Unusual, but true, that's what happened in when Kamala Harris ran for California attorney general in 2010. The race was so tight it took about a month for the final results to be counted and certified.

Initially, the Republican candidate thought he had won, but that was not the case.

In the end, Democrat Kamala Harris, the San Francisco district attorney, defeated Republican Steve Cooley, the Los Angeles district attorney, by more than 50,000 votes, or less than 1 percent of the vote.

> "...THEY LOOK TO US, TO SEE WHAT INNOVATION CAN BE. THEY LOOK TO US, BECAUSE WE ARE UNBURDENED BY WHAT HAS BEEN AND INSTEAD ARE INSPIRED BY WHAT CAN BE."
>
> – *Attorney General Kamala Harris, in her 2015 Inaugural Address, describing California's role as a leader in the country*

Attorney General Harris was sworn in on January 3, 2011, using a Bible held by her sister Maya.

That may sound like a big number, but more than 9.5 million votes were cast for that race. The win was historic. Harris became the first female, first African American, and first Indian American attorney general in California history!

In 2014, Attorney General Harris ran for a second term against attorney Ronald Gold, the Republican candidate. This time, she won easily by more than a million votes.

The attorney general, in every state, including California, functions as the top attorney who is in charge of enforcing the laws.

As noted on the website for the Office of the Attorney General for the State of California, "responsibilities include safeguarding the public from violent criminals, preserving California's spectacular natural resources, enforcing civil rights laws, and helping victims of identity theft, **mortgage**-related fraud, illegal business practices, and other consumer crimes." It's a big job, with California's attorney general "overseeing more than 4,500 lawyers, investigators, sworn peace officers, and other employees."

Her achievements as California attorney general include fighting fraud and drug trafficking, defending homeowners' rights, supporting marriage equality, and protecting the environment.

Leading the fight against cyberbullying has been another major achievement for Harris. To get input, she spoke with students, administrators, teachers, and police officers, including this visit to Peterson Middle School in Sunnyvale, California, in 2011.

"GETTING SMART ON CRIME DOES NOT MEAN REDUCING SENTENCES OR PUNISHMENTS FOR CRIMES."

— *Kamala Harris (2010),* Smart on Crime

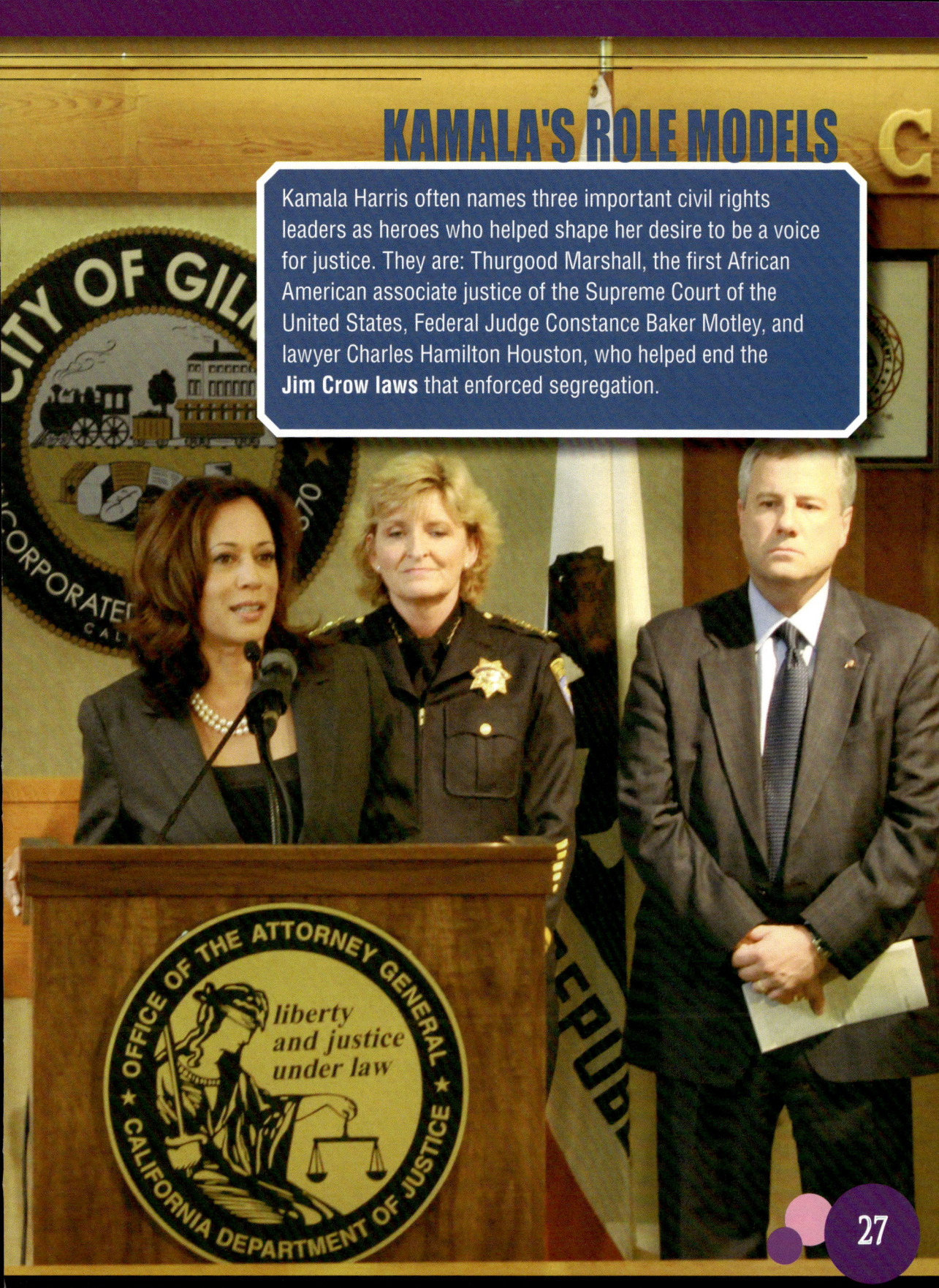

KAMALA'S ROLE MODELS

Kamala Harris often names three important civil rights leaders as heroes who helped shape her desire to be a voice for justice. They are: Thurgood Marshall, the first African American associate justice of the Supreme Court of the United States, Federal Judge Constance Baker Motley, and lawyer Charles Hamilton Houston, who helped end the **Jim Crow laws** that enforced segregation.

Homeowners discussed the mortgage fraud crisis and shared their stories at a 2011 roundtable with Harris.

FIGHTING FOR HOMEOWNERS' RIGHTS

From the moment Attorney General Kamala Harris took office in 2012, she pledged to fight for homeowners. In her **inaugural address**, she said, "…With over two million unemployed workers and the third worst foreclosure rate in the country, too many of our people are hurting." She said for many Californians, the dream of owning a home had turned into a nightmare. She added, "We will aggressively pursue any companies and individuals scamming innocent homeowners with mortgage fraud and false 'rescue' services that rob Californians of their assets and their dignity."

LOAN CRISIS

What was the subprime mortgage crisis? Maybe you heard about the financial crisis that caused millions of homeowners to lose their homes, particularly from 2007 to 2010. Subprime mortgages were a type of home loan that became popular in the early and mid-2000s, according to the **Federal Reserve** History website. "These high-risk mortgages became available from lenders (or banks) who funded mortgages by repackaging them into pools that were sold to investors," the website explains. These mortgages were risky because they were given to people who wouldn't normally qualify for loans because they had low credit scores, or didn't have a high enough income, or a steady income, to allow them to pay back the loan. With the easy availability of mortgages, housing prices increased, often artificially so. "When high-risk mortgage borrowers could not make loan payments, they either sold their homes at a loss and paid off their mortgages, or borrowed more against higher market prices." Or they lost their home to foreclosure. As California's attorney general, Kamala Harris was a leader in fighting big banks and negotiating a huge national settlement that "provided cash payments to many homeowners."

And aggressively pursue is exactly what she did. According to her website, she won a whopping "$25-billion settlement for California homeowners hit by the foreclosure crisis…"

The National Mortgage Settlement involved five major banks: Ally Financial, Bank of America, Citibank, JPMorgan Chase, and Wells Fargo, according to a press release from the State of California Department of Justice, Office of the Attorney General.

> The National Mortgage Settlement was both a public and personal triumph for Kamala Harris, She was widely praised for the way she played hardball with big banks – and won a victory for the people.

California Governor Edmund (Jerry) Brown Jr. signed the Homeowner Bill of Rights into law as a delighted Kamala Harris and other supporters of the new laws looked on.

HOMEOWNER BILL OF RIGHTS

The California Homeowner Bill of Rights took effect on January 1, 2013. Attorney General Kamala Harris and her staff worked tirelessly for more than a year to convince legislators to pass the package of new laws designed to prevent the abuses that caused the mortgage crisis in the first place.

"For too long, struggling homeowners in California have been denied fairness and transparency when dealing with their lending institutions," said Harris. "These laws give homeowners new rights."

The Homeowner Bill of Rights was the third step in her strong response to the mortgage crisis. A task force was created in 2011 to investigate and prosecute mortgage fraud, followed by the huge National Mortgage Settlement in 2012.

PRISON OVERCROWDING

Prison overcrowding is an important issue challenging states across the country. The issue became front and center for California when the United States Supreme Court agreed with a lower court's decision that California must reduce its overpopulation of prisoners. The courts found that overcrowding denied inmates' rights and caused poor medical and mental health care, which violated the Eight Amendment of the U.S. Constitution. The case required California to reduce its number of inmates by about 46,000 people to ease prison overcrowding.

As a result, lawmakers passed the Criminal Justice Realignment Act of 2011, which "shifted responsibility for the incarceration and supervision of low-level, nonviolent offenders from the state prisons to California's 58 counties," Attorney General Kamala Harris said in a *Stanford News Report*. The attorney general was addressing law students in a special class, "Advanced Seminar on Criminal Law & Public Policy: A Research Practicum," which she taught in 2011, highlighting and seeking solutions for California's **recidivism** problem.

CRUEL AND UNUSUAL PUNISHMENT

The California prison case was called *Brown* (for Governor Jerry Brown) *v. Plata* (Marciano Plata, one of the prisoners). It is an example of how judges have applied the Eighth Amendment, which was written in the 1700s, to modern life.

The Eight Amendment was intended to protect citizens from excessive fines that they could not pay and to prohibit "cruel and unusual punishment" such as torture. Since the 1700s, Americans have been discussing and debating just what that phrase means, including how it should apply to prison conditions.

Inmates were packed into spaces like this old gym at California's San Quentin Prison in 2006. There was no room to hold programs to help them live successfully after release.

As a senator, Harris says she fights not only for Californians, but for the ideals of the nation.

CHAPTER 5

CALIFORNIA'S THIRD FEMALE U.S. SENATOR

Election years are exciting, and the media thrives in the years when our country has a presidential election. While the nation was focused on the presidential campaigns of Hillary Clinton and Donald Trump in 2016, there also were key elections for senators throughout the country.

In California, the Senate race made history as two Democrats were on the ballot for the same seat. New rules in the state required that the two ballot spots go to the two top **primary** winners, regardless of their party. By defeating Loretta Sanchez, Kamala Harris became the second African American woman to serve in the U.S. Senate, and for California, the state's first African American senator, and the first South Asian, or Indian, woman senator for the United States.

> "LET'S BE REALISTIC. IT'S EASIER TO SOW HATE AND DIVISION THAN IT IS TO OFFER PEOPLE A MEANINGFUL, SUSTAINING SOLUTION."
>
> – Senator Kamala Harris to journalist Abby Aguirre for Vogue magazine

More than two dozen family and friends, from all over the world, gathered for the ceremonial swearing-in of Senator Kamala Harris by Vice President Joe Biden (center).

Her early years in the Senate, where she is called a "freshman" senator, have been busy, passionate, and vocal on many issues including gun violence, **immigration**, and women's rights. Her passion is matched with her active and pragmatic involvement in the Democratic Party, but also in reaching across the aisle to work with Republicans.

Her bills are a diverse and powerful reflection of her beliefs and work ethic, touching on issues of the economy, health, education, and gun violence. From early on in her term, it was clear Senator Harris would likely be influencing powerful committees before many senior senators do.

Committees are the smaller working groups that are key to getting legislation to the Senate floor for a vote. Senator Harris already serves on several important committees: the Homeland Security and Government Affairs Committee, the Select Committee on Intelligence, the Committee on the Judiciary, and the Committee on the Budget.

> "EVERY SINGLE DECISION WE MAKE IN CONGRESS – EVERYTHING FROM HEALTH CARE TO TAXES – AFFECTS OUR CHILDREN'S FUTURE. WE CAN'T JUST THINK ABOUT THE SHORT-TERM; WE HAVE TO THINK ABOUT WHAT KIND OF FUTURE WE'RE LEAVING THEM."
>
> – *Office of Senator Kamala Harris / Twitter / April 29, 2018*

Douglas Emhoff held a leather-bound family Bible for the ceremonial oath administered to his wife, Senator Kamala Harris, by Vice President Joe Biden on January 3, 2017.

WHAT DOES THE SENATE DO?

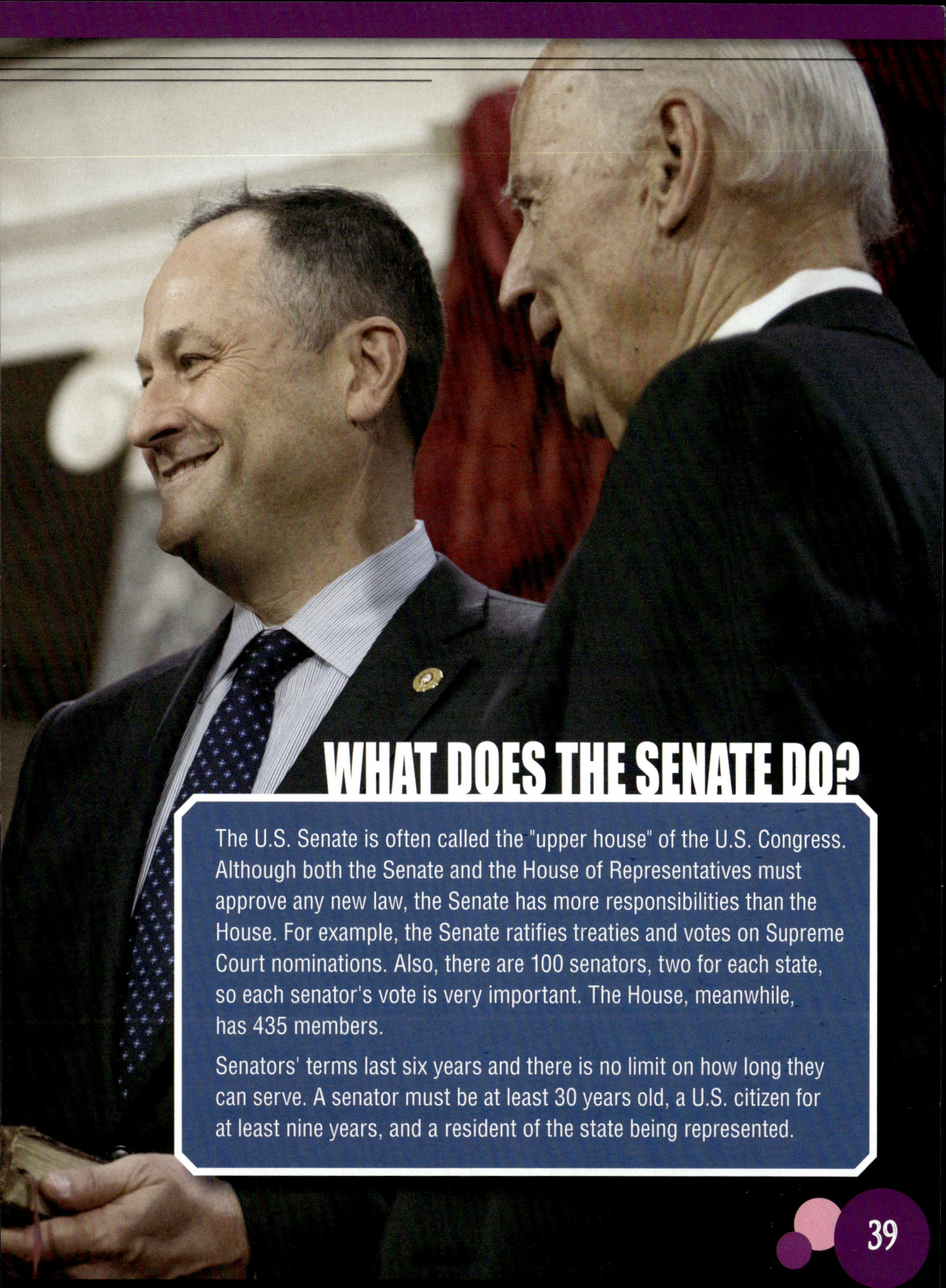

The U.S. Senate is often called the "upper house" of the U.S. Congress. Although both the Senate and the House of Representatives must approve any new law, the Senate has more responsibilities than the House. For example, the Senate ratifies treaties and votes on Supreme Court nominations. Also, there are 100 senators, two for each state, so each senator's vote is very important. The House, meanwhile, has 435 members.

Senators' terms last six years and there is no limit on how long they can serve. A senator must be at least 30 years old, a U.S. citizen for at least nine years, and a resident of the state being represented.

Senator Harris has kept true to her values and the issues that concern her most, and her **constituents** in California. She has co-sponsored a bill to battle the opioid crisis with Senator Bernie Sanders, an Independent from Vermont. But she also has been one of the co-writers of a bill with Senator Rand Paul, a Republican from Kentucky, to reform the criminal justice system on the issue of bail money. Bail allows people to stay out of jail by putting up money to guarantee they will appear for trial, but poor defendants often can't afford it.

Harris met with patients and staff at a Los Angeles treatment center for her research on the opioid crisis.

THE OPIOID EPIDEMIC

At least 115 Americans die every day in the United States from an opioid overdose, and experts say that number could triple by 2027. Opioids are a class of drugs that include heroin, fentanyl, and pain relievers available legally by prescription, such as oxycodone, hydrocodone, codeine, and morphine. In the 1990s, doctors wanted to do more to manage their patients' pain, especially back pain. Drug companies, eager to make money, assured them that people with legitimate pain would not get addicted to opioids.

They couldn't have been more wrong. By 2015, millions of people were addicted. It turns out that more than 20 percent of patients become abusers, and 4 to 6 percent move on to the illegal drug heroin.

More babies are being born addicted, more people are contracting diseases from sharing needles, and there isn't enough funding for treatment programs. Experts say 650,000 or more Americans are likely to die of opioid overdoses in the next decade unless drastic action is taken.

Drug overdoses kill more Americans each year than breast cancer, car crashes, or HIV/AIDS.

Harris has sponsored and introduced a bill, the Central Coast Heritage Act, to protect the coastal environment. She also sponsored a bill to protect and inform workers about any chemicals or pesticides they are handling in the workplace.

Harris frequently posts the progress of bills, and her own positions, on her Twitter account. Her tweets run from the sharp and savvy to passionate and praiseworthy. Mainly, as Harris has always done, she looks out for the underserved, fighting for rights with a mighty voice on these missions.

"HERE'S THE TRUTH PEOPLE NEED TO UNDERSTAND: TO TACKLE THE CHALLENGES OF THE 21ST CENTURY, WE MUST EMPOWER WOMEN AND GIRLS. IF WE DO NOT LIFT THEM UP, EVERYONE WILL FALL SHORT."

– Office of Senator Kamala Harris / Twitter / May 9, 2018

Helping constituents is an important part of a senator's job. Harris and California's other U.S. senator, Dianne Feinstein, went to Santa Rosa in October 2017 to urge residents to evacuate during a deadly wildfire. They said they would do everything possible to help with emergency federal aid.

GUN VIOLENCE

When thousands of students held a national walkout in April 2018, Senator Harris tweeted, "If it wasn't already clear, America's children won't stop marching & shouting until we do something to address the fact that kids are dying in their classrooms. Congress would be wise to listen."

The students were protesting mass shootings. As she was in California, Harris has been forthright in speaking about the issue in Washington. She believes more restrictions are needed on who can own guns and what kind of guns can be sold, along with other safety measures.

SHOOTING AT STONEMAN DOUGLAS HIGH SCHOOL

Seventeen people were shot to death and seventeen wounded on Valentine's Day 2018 at Marjory Stoneman Douglas High School in Parkland, Florida. A former student, 19-year-old Nikolas Cruz, confessed and could face the death penalty.

Though the school shooting was one of America's deadliest, Stoneman Douglas students fear it may be forgotten over time with nothing being done to stop gun violence. They formed a group called Never Again MSD to campaign for gun control and urged other students to join them. Rallies and protests have been held all over the country. Florida responded with a new package of laws approved in March. The laws raise the age for buying a rifle from 18 to 21, require waiting periods and background checks, allow for arming teachers, and beef up school security.

Students in the nation's capital heeded the call to action from Stoneman Douglas and organized a lie-in protest outside the White House on February 19, 2018.

Attorney General Harris led a 2011 sweep that took 1,209 guns from Californians who were barred from owning them. "We are all safer thanks to the sworn officers who carried out this sweep," she said.

As was noted in a press release one month after the mass shooting at Stoneman Douglas High School in Parkland, Florida, Senator Harris was an active speaker as a congressional committee held a hearing discussing ways to prevent such gun violence.

Harris pressed her fellow senators to work on this. She also was skeptical of a proposal by President Donald Trump that teachers be armed and trained to use firearms to prevent violence. To Senator Harris (and other senators), this would be impractical, as well as possibly dangerous. Instead, she has spoken out for other measures such as raising the age to 21 for owning a gun and renewing the assault weapon ban.

Senator Harris supports Dreamers by rallying with them and co-sponsoring the DREAM Act, which would help about a million young people.

SPEAKING UP FOR DREAMERS

Senator Harris has been unwavering in her support for immigrants, and particularly for young people brought to the U.S. illegally by their families as babies or toddlers. They are called Dreamers because a bill called the DREAM Act would let them stay and give them a path to citizenship.

She continues to meet and rally for policies to protect immigrants and work out their issues in California and the nation. She has spoken up repeatedly about travel bans, especially policies she believes target Muslim immigrants, or Muslim people who want to travel to visit families.

THE DACA ACT

DACA stands for Deferred Action for Childhood Arrivals. It is the name of the program President Barack Obama launched to ensure that those young people could continue growing up in the United States without fear of being sent back to their native country. Many of these children, of course, are now young adults and some even have young families of their own.

In her essay for *Elle* magazine, Senator Harris not only makes the point that the young people contribute to the richness of life here, she adds that the United States economy would "lose $460 billion over a decade."

Harris told Dreamers to stay strong and proud, and let people get to know them.

WOMEN'S MARCH ON WASHINGTON

Where were you on January 21, 2017? On that day, millions of women – some with their children and families – were out in full force across the United States to stand up on behalf of women's rights. The biggest march, or protest, was in Washington, D.C., where an estimated 2.6 million marched. Many smaller marches and rallies also took place across the country that day.

A day after the inauguration of President Donald Trump, the marches were held to send a message to the new administration that women – as well as men – could organize and empower voters to stand strong on all issues and stand up if women's rights were in danger.

In her address to those gathered in Washington, Senator Harris stressed that she doesn't get it when she is asked to speak on "women's issues." Crimes, security, and the economy – the issues of everyone – are issues for women, she pointed out. She also stressed optimism for the battles ahead and was critical of the inaugural message of the president, which she found pessimistic.

"WE ARE A FORCE THAT CANNOT BE DISMISSED OR WRITTEN OFF TO THE SIDELINES."
– Senator Harris addressing the Women's March on Washington, D.C.

TAKING ON TRUMP

Speaking about President Trump and his policies is something Senator Harris is very comfortable with. The president is not only a member of the opposition party, but also takes stands in sharp contrast to many of the issues the senator believes in and fights for.

Her first **rebuke** to the president came at the Women's March on Washington, and she has continued to speak out. She has been called a leader in the "resistance" to President Trump's policies.

Senator Harris rallied in support of Obamacare in June 2017. She tweeted, "Was outside the US Capitol to show GOP we won't stand by while they try to pass a bill that would leave 22M more Americans uninsured by 2026."

Families affected by President Donald Trump's travel ban told their stories to Senator Harris on February 21, 2017, in Van Nuys, California.

When the president gave his State of the Union address in 2018, an outline of his goals and upcoming policies, Harris was interviewed after the speech by a panel of Chris Matthews, Brian Williams, and Rachel Maddow on MSNBC. Harris emphasized that "the truth was lacking" in his speech. She mentioned that the president had talked about protecting Dreamers, but hadn't done this. She was particularly harsh and said "**fear mongering**" occurred when the president mentioned problems with undocumented immigrants and gangs in connection with policies for young people seeking to remain in the United States after being brought in as children.

Harris stood firm even when some male senators criticized her for asking tough questions of witnesses testifying in hearings.

CHAPTER 6

FUTURE PLANS

Senator Kamala Harris is already making her mark in Washington. As a first-term senator, she has been active and influential.

People have already been talking about a presidential bid for 2020. As of this writing, Senator Harris prefers to focus on issues and goals, as well as helping Democratic Party leaders get elected in every state.

She's a powerful fund-raiser, too, because of her popularity, accomplishments, and dynamic personality. Whether she's a guest on Stephen Colbert's show, doing a spot on *Ellen*, or in front of thousands at marches for justice, she excites and inspires a diverse group of viewers and followers.

> "I THINK WE MUST BE JOYFUL WARRIORS. LET'S BE JOYFUL WARRIORS. LET US UNDERSTAND THAT WE ARE NOT FIGHTING AGAINST SOMETHING, WE ARE FIGHTING FOR SOMETHING..."
>
> – Senator Harris at the 33rd annual Martin Luther King Jr. Kingdom Day Parade in Los Angeles

This has led many to speculate that down the road – whether it's 2020 or beyond, she would be an excellent candidate for the highest office.

She loves her home state of California, so there's always the possibility that someday she could seek to lead the Golden State as governor.

Her background as a lawyer, prosecutor, California attorney general, and now senator makes her uniquely qualified for a cabinet post or even a spot on the U.S. Supreme Court.

You could call her a superwoman, too, but her superpowers spring from a life of hard work, activism, and action. One thing is certain; anything is possible for this "joyful warrior."

"MY ADVICE TO BLACK GIRLS EVERYWHERE: WHENEVER YOU FIND YOURSELF IN A ROOM WHERE THERE AREN'T A LOT OF PEOPLE WHO LOOK LIKE YOU — BE IT A CLASSROOM, OR A BOARDROOM, OR A COURTROOM — REMEMBER THAT YOU HAVE AN ENTIRE COMMUNITY IN THAT ROOM WITH YOU, ALL OF US CHEERING YOU ON."

— *Office of Senator Kamala Harris / Twitter / March 18, 2018*

> "I'M ONE OF THE LUCKIEST PEOPLE ON EARTH."
> – Kamala Harris, interview with Sara Robinson, www.alternet.org, March 7, 2012

FAMILY LIFE

In 2014, Senator Harris married Douglas Emhoff, who also is a hardworking lawyer. As of this writing, he was a partner working at DLA Piper, in Century City, Los Angeles, and in Washington, D.C. According to the DLA Piper website, he is involved in "numerous community, civic and charitable activities that include legal aid, human rights, social justice and the well-being of children." Senator Harris is a proud stepmom to Cole and Ella, who are young adults.

Her sister Maya, besides being a lawyer and a public policy advocate, is on the board of directors for the Arcus Foundation, a group dedicated to promoting diversity and harmony in nature. Active in a variety of global philanthropies, Maya is married with a family.

Senator Harris's mother died in 2009, but the senator continues to mention her late mother as being an inspiration for all that she continues to do. Senator Harris's father is a professor emeritus at Stanford University in California.

Now happily married, Harris and Emhoff met on a blind date set up by one of her friends.

RECOGNITION

Senator Harris has focused on diverse issues with energy and persistence, which is reflected in her wide array of awards and recognition by various institutes, publications, and groups. Here are a few of the notable awards and recognitions she has received:

- 2018 Newsmaker of the Year Award, from the National Newspaper Publishers Association
- Commencement speaker, May 2018; invited by University of California, Berkeley students to return to the campus where her parents studied
- Honorary doctorate from Howard University, 2017
- 2017 "Global Thinker," recognized by *Foreign Policy* magazine

- 20/20 Bipartisan Justice Award, 2017
- President's Award at the Black Women's Agenda, Inc., 2017, 40th Annual Symposium Workshop and Awards Luncheon
- *Time* magazine's annual list of the 100 most influential people by the magazine, 2013
- Aspen-Rodel Fellow, Aspen Institute, 2006
- Top 100 Lawyers in California, 2006, *California Lawyer* magazine
- Thurgood Marshall Award, 2005, National Black Prosecutors Association
- Woman of Power, National Urban League, 2004

"TO OUR BROTHERS, SISTERS, AND FRIENDS IN IMMIGRANT COMMUNITIES AT HOME AND ACROSS THE WORLD, KNOW THAT WE STAND WITH YOU. IMMIGRANTS DON'T JUST BELONG IN AMERICA, IMMIGRANTS HAVE HELPED BUILD AMERICA."

Office of Senator Kamala Harris / Twitter / May 7, 2018

TIMELINE

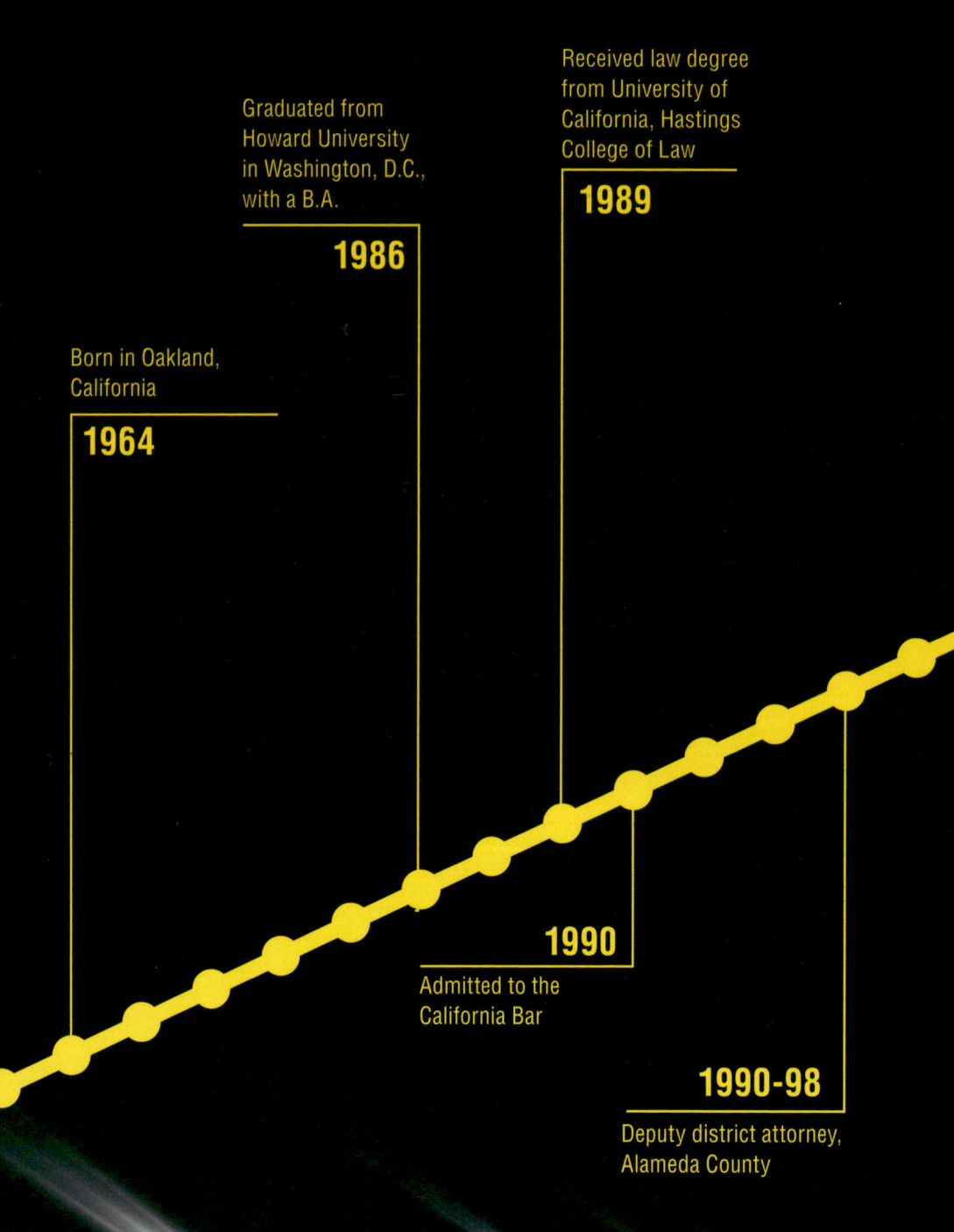

1964 — Born in Oakland, California

1986 — Graduated from Howard University in Washington, D.C., with a B.A.

1989 — Received law degree from University of California, Hastings College of Law

1990 — Admitted to the California Bar

1990-98 — Deputy district attorney, Alameda County

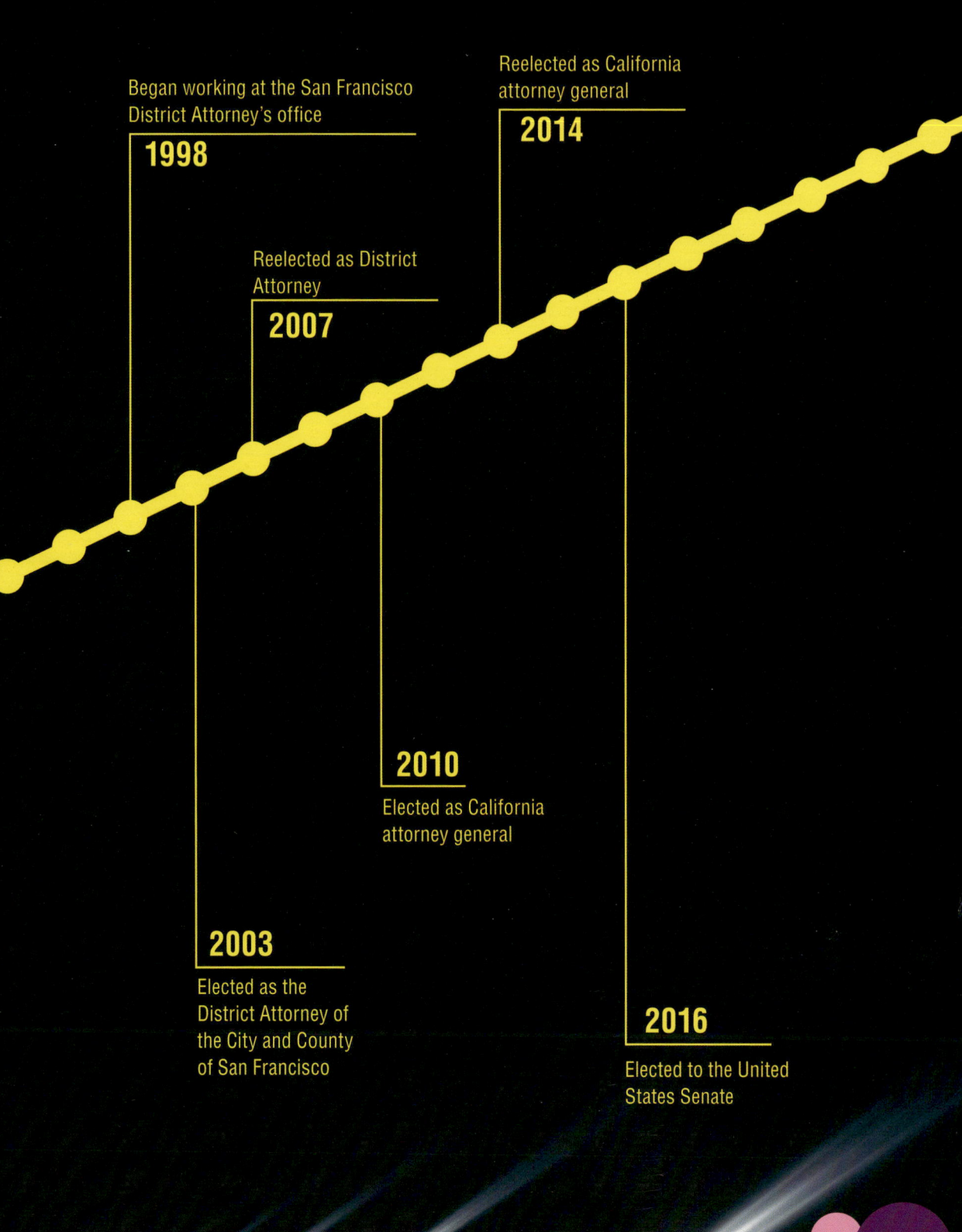

1998
Began working at the San Francisco District Attorney's office

2003
Elected as the District Attorney of the City and County of San Francisco

2007
Reelected as District Attorney

2010
Elected as California attorney general

2014
Reelected as California attorney general

2016
Elected to the United States Senate

GLOSSARY

constituents: People who live and vote in an area. In the U.S., for example, a senator's constituents are those voters in his or her state.

fear mongering: Creating a scary scenario, or frightening people at the possibility of an action leading to horrible outcomes. It is often not fact-based, and can include exaggeration or rumors that are not true.

Federal Reserve: The central bank of the United States, which sets monetary policy for the country.

hate crime: An assault or any other crime that is primarily motivated by a hatred or prejudice, targeting someone due to, for example, a person's skin color, ethnicity, religion, or gender.

immigration: When people travel from their homeland to a new country to establish a permanent home.

inaugural address: The speech a newly chosen official, such as the president or a governor, makes after they are inaugurated, or sworn in to the new office.

Jim Crow laws: Laws in states and cities designed to segregate people by the color of their skin, as well as bar them from participation in basic freedoms such as where to eat, sleep, shop, and vote.

LGBT: This is the commonly used abbreviation for lesbian, gay, bisexual, or transgender sexual orientation.

mortgage: A loan for a home by which the owner has bought the property, then pays the lender or bank a mortgage payment, usually monthly, to pay back the loan.

primary: Usually refers to an election during which members of the same political party run against one another for the opportunity to run in a major election. However, some primaries are nonpartisan.

rebuke: To be sharply critical and scold, or admonish someone for his or her actions or behavior.

recidivism: Used most often in connection with criminal behavior, when someone is back to committing crimes again after serving time in prison.

FOR MORE INFORMATION

BOOKS

Braun, Eric. *Loretta Lynch: First African American Woman Attorney General*. Minneapolis, MN: Lerner Publications, 2016.

Cooper, Ilene. *A Woman in the House (and Senate): How Women Came to the United States Congress, Broke Down Barriers, and Changed the Country*. New York, NY: Abrams Books for Young Readers, 2014.

WEBSITES

www.harris.senate.gov
This is the official U.S. Senate page of Kamala Harris.

www.rockthevote.org
This website focuses on voter registration for young people, but also has information on voting rights and action-oriented ideas on rallies and marches for the young activist.

INDEX

C
California bar, admitted to the 11
California Homeowner Bill of Rights 31
Central Coast Heritage Act 42
civil rights 5, 9, 10, 11, 25, 27
Criminal Justice Realignment Act of 2011 32
cyberbullying 25

D
Deferred Action for Childhood Arrivals (DACA act) 47
Democratic Party 7, 11, 37, 53
District Attorney 3, 5, 14, 15, 16, 23, 61
Dreamers 46, 47, 51

E
Emhoff, Douglas 38, 57, 61

G
gun violence 43

H
Harris, Donald 9
Harris, Maya 10, 24, 57
Harris, Shyamala Gopalan 9, 11, 57
Howard University 5, 11, 13, 58, 60

N
National Mortgage Settlement 30, 31

O
Oakland, California 5, 9, 60
opioid epidemic 41

S
social justice 5, 10, 57
Stoneman Douglas High School 44, 45

U
United States Senate 5, 10, 35, 37, 39, 61, 63
University of California, Hastings College of the Law 5, 9, 11, 14, 58, 60

W
Women's March On Washington 48, 49, 50

In putting together this book, the authors immersed themselves in all things Senator Harris, including listening to and reading her speeches, and watching TV interviews and talk show appearances and posted videos online. They also read dozens of articles about Harris, including newspaper profiles, magazine features, essays, and news stories, as well as *Smart on Crime: A Career Prosecutor's Plan to Make Us Safer*, by Kamala Harris with Joan O'C. Hamilton. They found a wealth of information on the State of California's Office of the Attorney General's website at https://oag.ca.gov, which has an archive of press releases and news. Additionally, Senator Harris's U.S. Senate website at www.harris.senate.gov provided important information and press releases. Here are the major resources that guided this project.

"8 Things to Know about Senate Candidate Kamala Harris' Career Gold Stars and Demerits.". http://www.latimes.com/politics/la-pol-ca-senate-harris-milestones-20160706-snap-htmlstory.html.

"10 Things You Didn't Know About Kamala Harris." *US News & World Report*. https://www.usnews.com/news/politics/articles/2017-06-20/10-things-you-didnt-know-about-kamala-harris.

"About the Office of the Attorney General." State of California - Department of Justice - Office of the Attorney General, January 20, 2011. https://oag.ca.gov/office.

Affairs, Public, UC Berkeley. "Kamala Harris to Give UC Berkeley's 2018 Commencement Address." Berkeley News, March 13, 2018. http://news.berkeley.edu/2018/03/13/senator-kamala-harris-to-give-uc-berkeleys-2018-commencement-address/.

Aguirre, Abby. "Dreaming Big: After a Year in Washington, Kamala Harris Has Proved She Doesn't Back down from a Fight. How Far Can the Star Senator Go?" *Vogue*, 2018.

"At 2.6 Million Strong, Women's Marches Crush Expectations." *USA TODAY*. Accessed May 1, 2018. https://www.usatoday.com/story/news/politics/2017/01/21/womens-march-aims-start-movement-trump-inauguration/96864158/.

"Attorney General Kamala D. Harris Inaugural Remarks," n.d., 5.

"Attorney General Kamala D. Harris Sworn In, Delivers Inaugural Address." State of California - Department of Justice - Office of the Attorney General, January 5, 2015. https://oag.ca.gov/news/press-releases/attorney-general-kamala-d-harris-sworn-delivers-inaugural-address.

Bazelon, Emily. "Kamala Harris, a 'Top Cop' in the Era of Black Lives Matter." *The New York Times*, May 25, 2016, sec. Magazine. https://www.nytimes.com/2016/05/29/magazine/kamala-harris-a-top-cop-in-the-era-of-black-lives-matter.html.

Cadei, Emily. "She Has Her Eye on 2020 and Trump. But First This California Senator Is Lending a Hand in 2018." The *Sacramento Bee*, April 13, 2018. http://www.sacbee.com/news/politics-government/capitol-alert/article208763234.html.

"California Attorney General Kamala Harris Plans to Be America's Next Black Female Senator," Essence.com." https://www.essence.com/2016/01/13/california-attorney-general-kamala-harris-americas-next-black-female-senator.

Carolyn Lochhead. "Kamala Harris Faces High Expectations as California's New Senator," *San Francisco Chronicle*." https://www.sfchronicle.com/politics/article/Kamala-Harris-faces-high-expectations-as-10831315.php.

"Cooley Concedes California Attorney General Race." *The Mercury News* (blog), November 24, 2010. https://www.mercurynews.com/2010/11/24/cooley-concedes-california-attorney-general-race/.

"Dr. Shyamala G. Harris's Obituary." San Francisco Chronicle. Accessed May 1, 2018. http://www.legacy.com/obituaries/sfgate/obituary.aspx?n=shyamala-g-harris&pid=125330757.

Driscoll, Sharon. "California Attorney General Kamala Harris Gives Public Talk at Stanford Law School." Stanford University, October 31, 2011. http://news.stanford.edu/news/2011/october/kamala-harris-law-103111.html.

Everett, Burgess, and Elana Schor. "Kamala Harris Keeps 'em Guessing.". POLITICO. http://politi.co/2FA7xIX.

"Fighting for Our Ideals." Kamala Harris, May 24, 2016. https://kamalaharris.org/2016/05/fighting-for-our-ideals/.

"Harris at MLK Parade: 'We Are Fighting for the Best of Who We Are' | U.S. Senator Kamala Harris of California." https://www.harris.senate.gov/news/press-releases/harris-at-mlk-parade-we-are-fighting-for-the-best-of-who-we-are.

Harris, Kamala. "Commencement Address at Howard University." Kamala Harris (blog), May 19, 2017. https://medium.com/@KamalaHarris/commencement-address-at-howard-university-704513cb0aec.

Harris, Kamala D. "Instead of 'One Size Fits All' Justice That Hurts Communities, Let's Get Smart on Crime." Huffington Post (blog), June 5, 2014. https://www.huffingtonpost.com/kamala-d-harris/instead-of-one-size-fits-_b_5453064.html.

"Sen. Kamala Harris: We Must Act to Protect Dreamers Before the New Year." *ELLE*, December 20, 2017. https://www.elle.com/culture/career-politics/a14473133/kamala-harris-dream-act-op-ed/.

Henderson, Nia-Malika. "Is Kamala Harris the next Barack Obama?" *Washington Post*, January 14, 2015, sec. The Fix. https://www.washingtonpost.com/news/the-fix/wp/2015/01/14/kamala-harris-democrats-next-big-thing/.

"How Race Helped Shape the Politics of Senate Candidate Kamala Harris." http://www.latimes.com/local/politics/la-me-pol-ca-harris-senate-20150930-story.html. Los Angeles Times.

Kamala D. Harris, and Joan O'C. Hamilton. *Smart on Crime: A Career Prosecutor's Plan to Make Us Safer*. Chronicle Books, 2009.

"Kamala Harris | United States Senator." Encyclopedia Britannica. https://www.britannica.com/biography/Kamala-Harris.

"Kamala Harris, California's Democratic Candidate for Attorney General, Refuses to Give Up." https://www.thedailybeast.com/kamala-harris-californias-democratic-candidate-for-attorney-general-refuses-to-give-up.

"Kamala Harris Declares Victory in AG's Race." *The Mercury News* (blog), November 30, 2010. https://www.mercurynews.com/2010/11/30/kamala-harris-declares-victory-in-ags-race-2/.

"Kamala Harris Emerges as Voice of Immigrant Advocates in the Senate." mcclatchydc. http://www.mcclatchydc.com/news/nation-world/national/article194342394.html.

"Kamala Harris Ends Pride Month with Inspiring Message for LGBT People," July 2, 2017. https://www.advocate.com/politics/2017/7/02/kamala-harris-ends-pride-month-inspiring-message-lgbt-people. The Advocate.

"Kamala Harris Navigates the 2020 Landscape." The Report/U.S. News." https://www.usnews.com/news/the-report/articles/2017-12-01/kamala-harris-navigates-the-2020-presidential-landscape.

"Kamala Harris: Women 'Are a Force That Cannot Be Dismissed.'" *Washington Post*. http://www.washingtonpost.com/video/kamala-harris-women-are-a-force-that-cannot-be-dismissed/2017/01/21/492746d8-e002-11e6-8902-610fe486791c_video.html.

"Kamala's Speech at the Human Rights Campaigns Annual Dinner." Kamala Harris, October 30, 2017. https://kamalaharris.org/2017/10/kamalas-speech-human-rights-campaigns-annual-dinner/.

"Mortgage Settlements: Homeowners." State of California - Department of Justice - Office of the Attorney General, February 8, 2012. https://oag.ca.gov/legal-opinions/ag-mortgage-settlements.

"My Story | U.S. Senator Kamala Harris of California." https://www.harris.senate.gov/about.

Nittle, Nadra Kareem. "This Groundbreaking Senator Has Been Called the Female Barack Obama." ThoughtCo. https://www.thoughtco.com/california-attorney-general-kamala-harris-2834885.

"'One on One' Rev. Al Sharpton Interview with Sen. Kamala Harris at the National Action Network." The Sharpton Primary. MSNBC, April 22, 2018.

"Recidivism in California." State of California - Department of Justice - Office of the Attorney General, September 21, 2016. https://oag.ca.gov/dap/evaluation/recidivism.

"Rising Democratic Party Star Kamala Harris Has Montreal Roots." CTV News." Accessed May 1, 2018. https://www.ctvnews.ca/canada/rising-democratic-party-star-kamala-harris-has-montreal-roots-1.3625032.

Roberts, Kayleigh. "Who Is Kamala Harris? 8 Things You Need to Know About the California Senator." *Cosmopolitan*, June 16, 2017. https://www.cosmopolitan.com/politics/a10025584/who-is-kamala-harris-facts/.

"Senator Kamala Harris Addresses Women's March Washington." https://www.c-span.org/video/?c4651431/senator-kamala-harris-addresses-womens-march-washington.

"Shut the Revolving Door of Prison." Brennan Center for Justice." https://www.brennancenter.org/analysis/shut-revolving-door-prison.

St. John, Paige. "Federal Judges Order California to Expand Prison Releases." latimes.com. http://www.latimes.com/local/political/la-me-ff-federal-judges-order-state-to-release-more-prisoners-20141114-story.html.

"Subprime Mortgage Crisis." Federal Reserve History." https://www.federalreservehistory.org/essays/subprime_mortgage_crisis.

"The Voter's Self Defense System." Vote Smart. http://votesmart.org.

"'Truth and Service': Kamala Harris Returns to Alma Mater, Howard, to Encourages Grads." NBC News. https://www.nbcnews.com/news/nbcblk/sen-kamala-harris-daughter-howard-university-comes-home-n758946.

"Two Democrats Will Face off for California's U.S. Senate Seat, Marking First Time a Republican Will Not Be in Contention." http://www.latimes.com/politics/la-pol-ca-senate-primary-election-20160607-snap-story.html.

"U.S. Senate Race: California's Kamala Harris Handily Beats Loretta Sanchez." *The Mercury News* (blog), November 3, 2016. https://www.mercurynews.com/2016/11/03/us-senate-race-harris-v-sanchez/.

"What's next for Kamala Harris?" The Washington Post." https://www.washingtonpost.com/news/the-fix/wp/2013/04/05/whats-next-for-kamala-harris/?noredirect=on&utm_term=.2b10f35f0574.Tang, Estelle.